Making All Things New

OTHER BOOKS BY HENRI J. M. NOUWEN

Henri J. M. Nouwen

Making All Things New

An Invitation to the Spiritual Life

HarperSanFrancisco
A Division of HarperCollinsPublishers

All Bible quotations are from the Jerusalem Bible.

HarperCollins books may be purchased for educational, business, or
sales promotional use. For information please write: Special Markets
Department, HarperCollins Publishers, 10 East 53rd Street,
New York, NY 10022.

HarperCollins Web Site: http://www.harpercollins.com
HarperCollins®, ☰®, and HarperSanFrancisco™ are trademarks of
HarperCollins Publishers Inc.

Designed by Catherine Hopkins

Library of Congress Cataloging-in-Publication Data
Nouwen, Henri J. M.
Making all things new.

1. Spiritual life—   I. Title.
BX2350.2.N674
248.4'82   80–8897
ISBN 0–06–066326–X

05 06 RRD H 50 49 48 47 46 45 44 43 42

In gratitude for
ten joyful years with
students and faculty of the
Yale Divinity School

Contents

Do not worry; do not say, "What are we to eat? What are we to drink? How are we to be clothed?" . . . Your heavenly Father knows you need them all. Set your hearts on his kingdom first . . . and all these other things will be given you as well.

—Matthew 6:31–33

ACKNOWLEDGMENTS

During the past few years, various friends have asked me, "What do you mean when you speak about the spiritual life?" Every time this question has come up, I have wished I had a small and simple book which could offer the beginning of a response. Although there are many excellent books about the spiritual life, I still felt that there was a place for a text which could be read within a few hours and could not only explain what the spiritual life is but also create a desire to live it. This feeling caused me to write this book. Many of the ideas have been expressed before by others as well as by myself, but I hope and pray that the way they are brought together here will be of help to those who feel "filled but unfulfilled."

I want to express my sincere thanks to the Passionist Sisters of Our Lady of Calvary retreat house in Farmington, Connecticut, who by their kindness and hospitality created the quiet space in which this book could be written. I am also grateful for the good advice and enthusiastic support of John Shopp and his colleagues at Harper & Row, and for the generous help of John Mogabgab, Robert Moore, and Wil Rikmanspoel in making the manuscript ready for publication. I owe a special word of thanks to the many students of the Yale Divinity School whose insightful criticisms on the first draft made me rewrite many parts of this text. Finally, I want to say thanks to Henry Morris, who suggested the title to me. I hope that all of us who worked together on this book will find that it was a worthwhile ministry.

INTRODUCTION

In this book I would like to explore what it means to live a spiritual life and how to live it. In the midst of our restless and hectic lives we sometimes wonder, "What is our true vocation in life?" "Where can we find the peace of mind to listen to the calling voice of God?" "Who can guide us through the inner labyrinth of our thoughts, emotions, and feelings?" These and many similar questions express a deep desire to live a spiritual life, but also a great unclarity about its meaning and practice.

I have written this book, first of all, for men and women who experience a persistent urge to enter more deeply into the spiritual life but are confused about the direction in which to go. These are the people who "know" the story of Christ and have a deep desire to let this knowledge descend from their minds into their hearts. They have a vague sense that such "heart-knowledge" can not only give them a new sense of who they are, but can even make all things new for them. But these same people often feel a certain hesitation and fear to enter on this uncharted path, and often wonder if they are not fooling themselves. I hope that, for them, this small book offers some encouragement and direction.

But I also want to speak, although indirectly, to the many for whom the Christian story is unfamiliar or strange but who experience a general desire for spiritual freedom. I hope that what is written for Christians is written in such a way that there is enough space for others to discover anchor-points in their own search for a spiritual home. This can only be a true book for Christians when it addresses itself also to those whose many questions about the meaning of life have remained open-ended. The authentic spiritual life finds its basis in the human condition, which all people—whether they are Christians or not—have in common.

As the point of departure, I have chosen Jesus' words "Do not worry." Worrying has become such a part and parcel of our daily life that a life without worries seems not only impossible, but even undesirable. We have a suspicion that to be carefree is unrealistic and —worse—dangerous. Our worries motivate us to work hard, to prepare ourselves for the future, and to arm ourselves against impending threats. Yet Jesus says, "Do not worry; do not say, 'What are we to eat? What are we to drink? How are we to be clothed?' . . . Your heavenly Father knows you need them all. Set your hearts on his kingdom first . . . and all these other things will be given you as well." With this radical and "unrealistic" counsel, Jesus points to the possibility of a life without worries, a life in which all things are being made new. Since I hope to describe the spiritual life in which the Spirit of God can recreate us as truly free people, I have called this book *Making All Things New.*

I have divided my reflections into three parts. In the first part, I want to discuss the destructive effects of worrying in our daily lives. In the second part, I plan to show how Jesus responds to our paralyzing worries by offering us a new life, a life in which the Spirit of God can make all things new for us. Finally, in the third part, I want to describe some specific disciplines which can cause our worries slowly to lose their grip on us, and which can thus allow the Spirit of God to do his recreating work.

1

"All These Other Things"

INTRODUCTION

The spiritual life is not a life before, after, or beyond our everyday existence. No, the spiritual life can only be real when it is lived in the midst of the pains and joys of the here and now. Therefore we need to begin with a careful look at the way we think, speak, feel, and act from hour to hour, day to day, week to week, and year to year, in order to become more fully aware of our hunger for the Spirit. As long as we have only a vague inner feeling of discontent with our present way of living, and only an indefinite desire for "things spiritual," our lives will continue to stagnate in a generalized melancholy. We often say, "I am not very happy. I am not content with the way my life is going. I am not really joyful or peaceful, but I just don't know how things can be different, and I guess I have to be realistic and accept my life as it is." It is this mood of resignation that prevents us from actively searching for the life of the Spirit.

Our first task is to dispel this vague, murky feeling of discontent and to look critically at how we are living our lives. This requires honesty, courage, and trust. We must honestly unmask and courageously confront our many self-deceptive games. We must trust that our honesty and courage will lead us not to despair, but to a new heaven and a new earth.

More so than the people of Jesus' day, we of

the "modern age" can be called worrying people. But how does our contemporary worrying actually manifest itself? Having looked critically at my own life and the lives of those around me, two words emerge as descriptive of our situation: filled and unfulfilled.

FILLED

One of the most obvious characteristics of our daily lives is that we are busy. We experience our days as filled with things to do, people to meet, projects to finish, letters to write, calls to make, and appointments to keep. Our lives often seem like overpacked suitcases bursting at the seams. In fact, we are almost always aware of being behind schedule. There is a nagging sense that there are unfinished tasks, unfulfilled promises, unrealized proposals. There is always something else that we should have remembered, done, or said. There are always people we did not speak to, write to, or visit. Thus, although we are very busy, we also have a lingering feeling of never really fulfilling our obligations.

The strange thing, however, is that it is very hard not to be busy. Being busy has become a status symbol. People expect us to be busy and to have many things on our minds. Often our friends say to us, "I guess you are busy, as usual," and mean it as a compliment. They reaffirm the general assumption that it is good to be busy. In fact, those who do not know what to do in the near future make their friends nervous. Being busy and being important often seem to mean the same thing. Quite a few telephone calls begin with the remark, "I know you are busy, but do you have a minute?"

suggesting that a minute taken from a person whose agenda is filled is worth more than an hour from someone who has little to do.

In our production-oriented society, being busy, having an occupation, has become one of the main ways, if not *the* main way, of identifying ourselves. Without an occupation, not just our economic security but our very identity is endangered. This explains the great fear with which many people face their retirement. After all, who are we when we no longer have an occupation?

More enslaving than our occupations, however, are our preoccupations. To be *pre*-occupied means to fill our time and place long before we are there. This is worrying in the more specific sense of the word. It is a mind filled with "ifs." We say to ourselves, "What if I get the flu? What if I lose my job? What if my child is not home on time? What if there is not enough food tomorrow? What if I am attacked? What if a war starts? What if the world comes to an end? What if . . . ?" All these "ifs" fill our minds with anxious thoughts and make us wonder constantly what to do and what to say in case something should happen in the future. Much, if not most, of our suffering is connected with these preoccupations. Possible career changes, possible family conflicts, possible illnesses, possible disasters, and a possible nuclear holocaust make us anxious, fearful, suspicious, greedy, nervous, and morose. They prevent us from feeling a real inner freedom. Since we are always preparing for eventualities, we seldom fully trust the moment. It is no exaggeration to say that much human energy is invested in these fearful preoccupations. Our individual as well as communal lives are so deeply molded by our worries about tomorrow that today hardly can be experienced.

Not only being occupied but also being preoccupied is highly encouraged by our society. The way in which newspapers, radio, and TV communicate their news to us creates an atmosphere of constant emergency. The excited voices of reporters, the predilection for gruesome accidents, cruel crimes, and perverted behavior, and the hour-to-hour coverage of human misery at home and abroad slowly engulf us with an all-pervasive sense of impending doom. On top of all this bad news is the avalanche of advertisements. Their unrelenting insistence that we will miss out on something very important if we do not read this book, see this movie, hear this speaker, or buy this new product deepens our restlessness and adds many fabricated preoccupations to the already existing ones.

Sometimes it seems as if our society has become dependent on the maintenance of these artificial worries. What would happen if we stopped worrying? If the urge to be entertained so much, to travel so much, to buy so much, and to arm ourselves so much no longer motivated our behavior, could our society as it is today still function? The tragedy is that we are indeed caught in a web of false expectations and contrived needs. Our occupations and preoccupations fill our external and internal lives to the brim. They prevent the Spirit of God from breathing freely in us and thus renewing our lives.

UNFULFILLED

Beneath our worrying lives, however, something else is going on. While our minds and hearts are filled with many things, and we wonder how we can live up to the expectations imposed upon us by ourselves and others, we have a deep sense of unfulfill-ment. While busy with and worried about many things, we seldom feel truly satisfied, at peace, or at home. A gnawing sense of being unfulfilled underlies our filled lives. Reflect-ing a little more on this experience of un-fulfillment, I can discern different senti-ments. The most significant are boredom, resentment, and depression.

Boredom is a sentiment of disconnected-ness. While we are busy with many things, we wonder if what we do makes any real difference. Life presents itself as a random and unconnected series of activities and events over which we have little or no con-trol. To be bored, therefore, does not mean that we have nothing to do, but that we question the value of the things we are so busy doing. The great paradox of our time is that many of us are busy and bored at the same time. While running from one event to the next, we wonder in our innermost selves if anything is really happening. While we can hardly keep up with our many tasks and obligations, we are not so sure that it would make any difference if we did nothing at all. While people keep pushing us in all directions, we doubt if anyone really cares. In short, while our lives are full, we feel unfulfilled.

Boredom is often closely linked to resentment. When we are busy, yet wondering if our busyness means anything to anyone, we easily feel used, manipulated, and exploited. We begin to see ourselves as victims pushed around and made to do all sorts of things by people who do not really take us seriously as human beings. Then an inner anger starts to develop, an anger which in time settles into our hearts as an always fretting companion. Our hot anger gradually becomes cold anger. This "frozen anger" is the resentment which has such a poisoning effect on our society.

The most debilitating expression of our unfulfillment, however, is depression. When we begin to feel not only that our presence makes little difference but also that our absence might be preferred, we can easily be engulfed by an overwhelming sense of guilt. This guilt is not connected with any particular action, but with life itself. We feel guilty being alive. The realization that the world might be better off without the soft drink, the deodorant, or the nuclear submarine, whose production fills the working hours of our life, can lead us to the despairing question, "Is my life worth living?" It is therefore not so surprising that people who are praised by many for their successes and accomplishments often feel very unfulfilled, even to the point of committing suicide.

Boredom, resentment, and depression are all sentiments of disconnectedness. They present life to us as a broken connection. They give us a sense of not-belonging. In interpersonal relations, this disconnectedness is experienced as loneliness. When we are lonely we perceive ourselves as isolated individuals surrounded, perhaps, by many people, but not really part of any supporting or nurturing community. Loneliness is without doubt one of the most widespread diseases of our time. It affects not only retired life but also family life, neighborhood life, school life, and business life. It causes suffering not only in elderly people but also in children, teenagers, and adults. It enters not only prisons but also private homes, office buildings, and hospitals. It is even visible in the diminishing interaction between people on the streets of our cities. Out of all this pervading loneliness many cry, "Is there anyone who really cares? Is there anyone who can take away my inner sense of isolation? Is there anyone with whom I can feel at home?"

It is this paralyzing sense of separation that constitutes the core of much human suffering. We can take a lot of physical and even mental pain when we know that it truly makes us a part of the life we live together in this world. But when we feel cut off from the human family, we quickly lose heart. As long as we believe that our pains and struggles connect us with our fellow men and women and thus make us part of the common human struggle for a better future, we are quite willing to accept a demanding task. But when we think of ourselves as passive bystanders who have no contribution to make to the story of life, our pains are no longer growing pains and our struggles no longer offer new life, because then we have a sense that our lives die out behind us and do not lead us anywhere. Sometimes, indeed, we have to say that the only thing we remember of our recent past is that we were very busy, that everything seemed very urgent, and that we could hardly get it all done. *What* we were doing we have forgotten. This shows how isolated we have become. The past no longer carries us to the future; it simply leaves us worried, without any promise that things will be different.

Our urge to be set free from this isolation can become so strong that it bursts forth in violence. Then our need for an intimate relationship—for a friend, a lover, or an appreciative community—turns into a desperate

grabbing for anyone who offers some immediate satisfaction, some release of tension, or
some temporary feeling of at-oneness. Then
our need for each other degenerates into a
dangerous aggression that causes much harm
and only intensifies our feelings of loneliness.

CONCLUSION

I hope that these reflections have
brought us a little closer to the meaning of
the word *worry* as it was used by Jesus. Today
worrying means to be occupied and preoccupied with many things, while at the same
time being bored, resentful, depressed, and
very lonely. I am not trying to say that all of
us are worried in such an extreme way all the
time. Yet, there is little doubt in my mind
that the experience of being filled yet un-

fulfilled touches most of us to some degree at some time. In our highly technological and competitive world, it is hard to avoid completely the forces which fill up our inner and outer space and disconnect us from our innermost selves, our fellow human beings, and our God.

One of the most notable characteristics of worrying is that it fragments our lives. The many things to do, to think about, to plan for, the many people to remember, to visit, or to talk with, the many causes to attack or defend, all these pull us apart and make us lose our center. Worrying causes us to be "all over the place," but seldom at home. One way to express the spiritual crisis of our time is to say that most of us have an address but cannot be found there. We know where we belong, but we keep being pulled away in many directions, as if we were still homeless.

"All these other things" keep demanding our attention. They lead us so far from home that we eventually forget our true address, that is, the place where we can be addressed.

Jesus responds to this condition of being filled yet unfulfilled, very busy yet unconnected, all over the place yet never at home. He wants to bring us to the place where we belong. But his call to live a spiritual life can only be heard when we are willing honestly to confess our own homeless and worrying existence and recognize its fragmenting effect on our daily life. Only then can a desire for our true home develop. It is of this desire that Jesus speaks when he says, "Do not worry. . . . Set your hearts on his kingdom first . . . and all these other things will be given you as well."

II

"His Kingdom First"

INTRODUCTION

Jesus does not respond to our worry-filled way of living by saying that we should not be so busy with worldly affairs. He does not try to pull us away from the many events, activities, and people that make up our lives. He does not tell us that what we do is unimportant, valueless, or useless. Nor does he suggest that we should withdraw from our involvements and live quiet, restful lives removed from the struggles of the world.

Jesus' response to our worry-filled lives is

quite different. He asks us to shift the point of gravity, to relocate the center of our attention, to change our priorities. Jesus wants us to move from the "many things" to the "one necessary thing." It is important for us to realize that Jesus in no way wants us to leave our many-faceted world. Rather, he wants us to live in it, but firmly rooted in the center of all things. Jesus does not speak about a change of activities, a change in contacts, or even a change of pace. He speaks about a change of heart. This change of heart makes everything different, even while everything appears to remain the same. This is the meaning of "Set your hearts on his kingdom first . . . and all these other things will be given you as well." What counts is where our hearts are. When we worry, we have our hearts in the wrong place. Jesus asks us to move our hearts to the center, where all other things fall into place.

What is this center? Jesus calls it the kingdom, the kingdom of his Father. For us of the twentieth century, this may not have much meaning. Kings and kingdoms do not play an important role in our daily life. But only when we understand Jesus' words as an urgent call to make the life of God's Spirit our priority can we see better what is at stake. A heart set on the Father's kingdom is also a heart set on the spiritual life. To set our hearts on the kingdom therefore means to make the life of the Spirit within and among us the center of all we think, say, or do.

I now want to explore in some depth this life in the Spirit. First we need to see how in Jesus' own life the Spirit of God manifests itself. Then we need to discern what it means for us to be called by Jesus to enter with him into this life of the Spirit.

JESUS' LIFE

There is little doubt that Jesus' life was a very busy life. He was busy teaching his disciples, preaching to the crowds, healing the sick, exorcising demons, responding to questions from foes and friends, and moving from one place to another. Jesus was so involved in activities that it became difficult to have any time alone. The following story gives us the picture: "They brought to him all who were sick and those who were possessed by devils. The whole town came crowding round the door, and he cured many who were suffering from diseases of one kind or another; he also cast out many devils. . . . In the morning, long before dawn, he got up and left the house, and went off to a lonely place and prayed there. Simon and his companions set out in search of him, and when they found him they said, 'Everybody is looking for you.' He answered, 'Let us go elsewhere, to the neighboring country towns, so that I can preach there too, because that is why I came.' And he went all through Galilee, preaching in their synagogues and casting out devils" (Mark 1:32–39).

It is clear from this account that Jesus had a very filled life and was seldom if ever left alone. He might even appear to us as a fanatic driven by a compulsion to get his message across at any cost. The truth, however, is different. The deeper we enter into the Gospel accounts of his life, the more we see that Jesus was not a zealot trying to accomplish many different things in order to reach a self-imposed goal. On the contrary, everything we know about Jesus indicates that he was concerned with only one thing: to do the will of his Father. Nothing in the Gospels is as impressive as Jesus' single-minded obedience to his Father. From his first recorded words in the Temple, "Did you not know that I must be busy with my Father's affairs?" (Luke 2:49), to his last words on the cross, "Father, into your hands I commit my spirit" (Luke 23:46), Jesus' only concern was to do the will of his Father. He says, "The Son can do nothing by himself; he can do only what he sees the Father doing" (John 5:19). The works Jesus did are the works the Father sent him to do, and the words he spoke are the words the Father gave him. He leaves no doubt about this: "If I am not doing my Father's work, there is no need to believe me . . ." (John 10:37); "My word is not my own; it is the word of the one who sent me" (John 14:24).

Jesus is not our Savior simply because of

what he said to us or did for us. He is our Savior because what he said and did was said and done in obedience to his Father. That is why St. Paul could say, "As by one man's disobedience many were made sinners, so by one man's obedience many will be made righteous" (Romans 5:19). Jesus is the obedient one. The center of his life is this obedient relationship with the Father. This may be hard for us to understand, because the word *obedience* has so many negative connotations in our society. It makes us think of authority figures who impose their wills against our desires. It makes us remember unhappy childhood events or hard tasks performed under threats of punishment. But none of this applies to Jesus' obedience. His obedience means a total, fearless listening to his loving Father. Between the Father and the Son there is only love. Everything that belongs to the Father, he entrusts to the Son (Luke 10:22), and everything the Son has received, he returns to the Father. The Father opens himself totally to the Son and puts everything in his hands: all knowledge (John 12:50), all glory (John 8:54), all power (John 5:19–21). And the Son opens himself totally to the Father and thus returns everything into his Father's hands. "I came from the Father and have come into the world and now I leave the world to go to the Father" (John 16:28).

This inexhaustible love between the Father and the Son includes and yet transcends all forms of love known to us. It includes the love of a father and mother, a brother and sister, a husband and wife, a teacher and friend. But it also goes far beyond the many limited and limiting human experiences of love we know. It is a caring yet demanding love. It is a supportive yet severe love. It is a gentle yet strong love. It is a love that gives life yet accepts death. In this divine love Jesus was sent into the world, to this divine love Jesus offered himself on the cross. This all-embracing love, which epitomizes the relationship between the Father and the Son, is a divine Person, coequal with the Father and the Son. It has a personal name. It is called the Holy Spirit. The Father loves the Son and pours himself out in the Son. The Son is loved by the Father and returns all he is to the Father. The Spirit is love itself, eternally embracing the Father and the Son.

This eternal community of love is the center and source of Jesus' spiritual life, a life of uninterrupted attentiveness to the Father in the Spirit of love. It is from this life that Jesus' ministry grows. His eating and fasting, his praying and acting, his traveling and resting, his preaching and teaching, his exorcising and healing, were all done in this Spirit of love. We will never understand the full meaning of Jesus' richly varied ministry unless we see how the many things are rooted in the one thing: listening to the Father in the intimacy of perfect love. When we see this, we will also realize that the goal of Jesus' ministry is nothing less than to bring us into this most intimate community.

OUR LIVES

Our lives are destined to become like the life of Jesus. The whole purpose of Jesus' ministry is to bring us to the house of his Father. Not only did Jesus come to free us from the bonds of sin and death, he also came to lead us into the intimacy of his divine life. It is difficult for us to imagine what this means. We tend to emphasize the distance between Jesus and ourselves. We see Jesus as the all-knowing and all-powerful Son of God who is unreachable for us sinful, broken human beings. But in thinking this way, we forget that Jesus came to give us his own life. He came to lift us up into loving community with the Father. Only when we recognize the radical purpose of Jesus' ministry will we be able to understand the meaning of the spiritual life. Everything that belongs to Jesus is given for us to receive. All that Jesus does we may also do. Jesus does not speak about us as second-class citizens. He does not withhold anything from us: "I have made known to you everything I have learned from my Father" (John 15:15); "Whoever believes in me will perform the same works as I do myself" (John 14:12). Jesus wants us to be where he is. In his priestly prayer, he leaves no doubt about his intentions: "Father, may they be one in us, as you are in me and I am in you. . . . I have given them the glory you gave to me, that they may be one as we are one. With me in them and you in me, may they be so completely one that the world will realize . . . that I have loved them as much as you loved me. Father, I want those you have given me to be with me where I am, so that they may always see the glory you have given me. . . . I have made your name known to them and will continue to make it known, so that the love with which you loved me may be in them, and so that I may be in them" (John 17:21–26).

These words beautifully express the nature of Jesus' ministry. He became like us so that we might become like him. He did not cling to his equality with God, but emptied himself and became as we are so that we might become like him and thus share in his divine life.

This radical transformation of our lives is the work of the Holy Spirit. The disciples could hardly comprehend what Jesus meant. As long as Jesus was present to them in the flesh, they did not yet recognize his full presence in the Spirit. That is why Jesus said: "It is for your own good that I am going because unless I go, the Advocate [the Holy Spirit] will not come to you; but if I do go, I will send him to you. . . . When the Spirit of truth comes he will lead you to the complete truth, since he will not be speaking as from himself but will say only what he has learned; and he will tell you of the things to come. He will glorify me, since all he tells you will be taken from what is mine. Everything the Father has is mine; that is why I said: All he tells you will be taken from what is mine" (John 16:7, 13–15).

Jesus sends the Spirit so that we may be led to the full truth of the divine life. *Truth* does not mean an idea, concept, or doctrine, but the true relationship. To be led into the truth is to be led into the same relationship that Jesus has with the Father; it is to enter into a divine betrothal.

Thus Pentecost is the completion of Jesus' mission. On Pentecost the fullness of Jesus' ministry becomes visible. When the Holy Spirit descends upon the disciples and dwells with them, their lives are transformed into Christ-like lives, lives shaped by the same love that exists between the Father and the Son. The spiritual life is indeed a life in which we are lifted up to become partakers of the divine life.

To be lifted up into the divine life of the

Father, the Son, and the Holy Spirit does not mean, however, to be taken out of the world. On the contrary, those who have entered into the spiritual life are precisely the ones who are sent into the world to continue and fulfill the work that Jesus began. The spiritual life does not remove us from the world but leads us deeper into it. Jesus says to his Father, "As you sent me into the world, I have sent them into the world" (John 17:18). He makes it clear that precisely because his disciples no longer belong to the world, they can live in the world as he did: "I am not asking you to remove them from the world, but to protect them from the evil one. They do not belong to the world any more than I belong to the world" (John 17:15–16). Life in the Spirit of Jesus is therefore a life in which Jesus' coming into the world—his incarnation, his death, and resurrection—is lived out by those who have entered into the same obedient relationship to the Father which marked Jesus' own life. Having become sons and daughters as Jesus was Son, our lives become a continuation of Jesus' mission.

"Being in the world without being of the world." These words summarize well the way Jesus speaks of the spiritual life. It is a life in which we are totally transformed by the Spirit of love. Yet it is a life in which everything seems to remain the same. To live a spiritual life does not mean that we must leave our families, give up our jobs, or change our ways of working; it does not mean that we have to withdraw from social or political activities, or lose interest in literature and art; it does not require severe forms of asceticism or long hours of prayer. Changes such as these may in fact grow out of our spiritual life, and for some people radical decisions may be necessary. But the spiritual life can be lived in as many ways as there are people. What is new is that we have moved from the many things to the kingdom of God. What is new is that we are set free from the compulsions of our world and have set our hearts on the only necessary thing. What is new is that we no longer experience the many things, people, and events as endless causes for worry, but begin to experience them as the rich variety of ways in which God makes his presence known to us.

Indeed, living a spiritual life requires a change of heart, a conversion. Such a conversion may be marked by a sudden inner change, or it can take place through a long, quiet process of transformation. But it always involves an inner experience of oneness. We realize that we are in the center, and that from there all that is and all that takes place can be seen and understood as part of the mystery of God's life with us. Our conflicts and pains, our tasks and promises, our families and friends, our activities and projects, our hopes and aspirations, no longer appear to us as a fatiguing variety of things which we can barely keep together, but rather as affirmations and revelations of the new life of the Spirit in us. "All these other things," which so occupied and preoccupied us, now come as gifts or challenges that strengthen and deepen the new life which we have discovered. This does not mean that the spiritual life makes things easier or takes our struggles and pains away. The lives of Jesus' disciples clearly show that suffering does not diminish because of conversion. Sometimes it even becomes more intense. But our attention is no longer directed to the "more or less." What matters is to listen attentively to the

Spirit and to go obediently where we are being led, whether to a joyful or a painful place.

Poverty, pain, struggle, anguish, agony, and even inner darkness may continue to be part of our experience. They may even be God's way of purifying us. But life is no longer boring, resentful, depressing, or lonely because we have come to know that everything that happens is part of our way to the house of the Father.

CONCLUSION

"His kingdom first." I hope that these words have received some new meaning. They call us to follow Jesus on his obedient way, to enter with him into the community established by the demanding love of the

Father, and to live all of life from there. The kingdom is the place where God's Spirit guides us, heals us, challenges us, and renews us continuously. When our hearts are set on that kingdom, our worries will slowly move to the background, because the many things which made us worry so much start to fall into place. It is important to realize that "setting your heart on the kingdom" is not a method for winning prizes. In that case the spiritual life would become like winning the jackpot on a TV game show. The words "all other things will be given you as well" express that indeed God's love and care extend to our whole being. When we set our hearts on the life in the Spirit of Christ, we will come to see and understand better how God keeps us in the palm of his hand. We will come to a better understanding of what we truly need for our physical and mental well-being, and we will come to experience the intimate connections between our spiritual life and our temporal needs while journeying through his world.

But this leaves us with a very difficult question. Is there a way to move from our worry-filled life to the life of the Spirit? Must we simply wait passively until the Spirit comes along and blows away our worries? Are there any ways by which we can prepare ourselves for the life of the Spirit and deepen that life once it has touched us? The distance between the filled yet unfulfilled life on the one hand, and the spiritual life on the other, is so great that it may seem quite unrealistic to expect to move from one to another. The claims that daily living makes on us are so real, so immediate, and so urgent that a life in the Spirit seems beyond our capabilities.

My description of the worry-filled life and

the spiritual life as the two extremes of the spectrum of living was necessary to make clear what is at stake. But most of us are neither worrying constantly nor absorbed solely in the Spirit. Often there are flashes of the presence of God's Spirit in the midst of our worries, and often worries arise even when we experience the life of the Spirit in our innermost self. It is important that we gradually realize where we are and learn how we can let the life of God's Spirit grow stronger in us.

This brings me to the final task: to describe the main disciplines which can support us in our desire to have our worries lose their grip on us, and to let the Spirit guide us to the true freedom of the children of God.

III

"Set Your Hearts"

INTRODUCTION

The spiritual life is a gift. It is the gift of the Holy Spirit, who lifts us up into the kingdom of God's love. But to say that being lifted up into the kingdom of love is a divine gift does not mean that we wait passively until the gift is offered to us. Jesus tells us to set our hearts on the kingdom. Setting our hearts on something involves not only serious aspiration but also strong determination. A spiritual life requires human effort. The forces that keep pulling us back into a worry-filled life are far from easy to overcome.

"How hard it is," Jesus exclaims, ". . . to enter the kingdom of God!" (Mark 10:23). And to convince us of the need for hard work, he says, "If anyone wants to be a follower of mine, let him renounce himself and take up his cross and follow me" (Matthew 16:24).

Here we touch the question of discipline in the spiritual life. A spiritual life without discipline is impossible. Discipline is the other side of discipleship. The practice of a spiritual discipline makes us more sensitive to the small, gentle voice of God. The prophet Elijah did not encounter God in the mighty wind or in the earthquake or in the fire, but in the small voice (see 1 Kings 19:9–13). Through the practice of a spiritual discipline we become attentive to that small voice and willing to respond when we hear it.

From all that I said about our worried, over-filled lives, it is clear that we are usually surrounded by so much inner and outer noise that it is hard to truly hear our God when he is speaking to us. We have often become deaf, unable to know when God calls us and unable to understand in which direction he calls us. Thus our lives have become absurd. In the word *absurd* we find the Latin word *surdus,* which means "deaf." A spiritual life requires discipline because we need to learn to listen to God, who constantly speaks but whom we seldom hear. When, however, we learn to listen, our lives become obedient lives. The word *obedient* comes from the Latin word *audire,* which means "listening." A spiritual discipline is necessary in order to move slowly from an absurd to an obedient life, from a life filled with noisy worries to a life in which there is some free inner space where we can listen to our God and follow his guidance. Jesus' life was a life of obedience. He was always listening to the Father, always attentive to his voice, always alert for his directions. Jesus was "all ear." That is true prayer: being all ear for God. The core of all prayer is indeed listening, obediently standing in the presence of God.

A spiritual discipline, therefore, is the concentrated effort to create some inner and outer space in our lives, where this obedience can be practiced. Through a spiritual discipline we prevent the world from filling our lives to such an extent that there is no place left to listen. A spiritual discipline sets us free to pray or, to say it better, allows the Spirit of God to pray in us.

I will now present two disciplines through which we can "set our hearts on the kingdom." They can be considered as disciplines of prayer. They are the discipline of solitude and the discipline of community.

SOLITUDE

Without solitude it is virtually impossible to live a spiritual life. Solitude begins with a time and place for God, and him alone. If we really believe not only that God exists but also that he is actively present in our lives—healing, teaching, and guiding— we need to set aside a time and space to give him our undivided attention. Jesus says, "Go to your private room and, when you have shut your door, pray to your Father who is in that secret place" (Matthew 6:6).

To bring some solitude into our lives is one of the most necessary but also most difficult disciplines. Even though we may have a deep desire for real solitude, we also experience a certain apprehension as we approach that solitary place and time. As soon as we are alone, without people to talk with, books to read, TV to watch, or phone calls to make, an inner chaos opens up in us. This chaos can be so disturbing and so confusing that we can hardly wait to get busy again. Entering a private room and shutting the door, therefore, does not mean that we immediately shut out all our inner doubts, anxieties, fears, bad memories, unresolved conflicts, angry feelings, and impulsive desires. On the contrary, when we have removed our outer distractions, we often find that our inner distractions manifest themselves to us in full force. We often use the outer distractions to shield ourselves from the interior noises. It is thus not surprising that we have a difficult time being alone. The confrontation with our inner conflicts can be too painful for us to endure.

This makes the discipline of solitude all the more important. Solitude is not a spontaneous response to an occupied and preoccupied life. There are too many reasons not to be alone. Therefore we must begin by carefully planning some solitude. Five or ten minutes a day may be all we can tolerate. Perhaps we are ready for an hour every day, an afternoon every week, a day every month, or a week every year. The amount of time will vary for each person according to temperament, age, job, lifestyle, and maturity. But we do not take the spiritual life seriously if we do not set aside some time to be with God and listen to him. We may have to write it in black and white in our daily calendar so that nobody else can take away this period of time. Then

we will be able to say to our friends, neighbors, students, customers, clients, or patients,
"I'm sorry, but I've already made an appoint-
ment at that time and it can't be changed."

Once we have committed ourselves to
spending time in solitude, we develop an attentiveness to God's voice in us. In the beginning, during the first days, weeks, or even
months, we may have the feeling that we are
simply wasting our time. Time in solitude
may at first seem little more than a time in
which we are bombarded by thousands of
thoughts and feelings that emerge from hid-
den areas of our mind. One of the early
Christian writers describes the first stage of
solitary prayer as the experience of a man
who, after years of living with open doors,
suddenly decides to shut them. The visitors
who used to come and enter his home start
pounding on his doors, wondering why they

are not allowed to enter. Only when they realize that they are not welcome do they gradually stop coming. This is the experience of anyone who decides to enter into solitude after a life without much spiritual discipline. At first, the many distractions keep presenting themselves. Later, as they receive less and less attention, they slowly withdraw.

It is clear that what matters is faithfulness to the discipline. In the beginning, solitude seems so contrary to our desires that we are constantly tempted to run away from it. One way of running away is daydreaming or simply falling asleep. But when we stick to our discipline, in the conviction that God is with us even when we do not yet hear him, we slowly discover that we do not want to miss our time alone with God. Although we do not experience much satisfaction in our solitude, we realize that a day without solitude is less "spiritual" than a day with it.

Intuitively, we know that it is important to spend time in solitude. We even start looking forward to this strange period of uselessness. This desire for solitude is often the first sign of prayer, the first indication that the presence of God's Spirit no longer remains unnoticed. As we empty ourselves of our many worries, we come to know not only with our mind but also with our heart that we never were really alone, that God's Spirit was with us all along. Thus we come to understand what Paul writes to the Romans, "Sufferings bring patience . . . and patience brings perseverance, and perseverance brings hope, and this hope is not deceptive, because the love of God has been poured into our hearts by the Holy Spirit which has been given to us" (Romans 5:4–6). In solitude, we come to know the Spirit who has already been given to us. The pains and struggles we encounter in our solitude thus become the way to hope, because our hope is not based on something that will happen after our sufferings are over, but on the real presence of God's healing Spirit in the midst of these sufferings. The discipline of solitude allows us gradually to come in touch with this hopeful presence of God in our lives, and allows us also to taste even now the beginnings of the joy and peace which belong to the new heaven and the new earth.

The discipline of solitude, as I have described it here, is one of the most powerful disciplines in developing a prayerful life. It is a simple, though not easy, way to free us from the slavery of our occupations and preoccupations and to begin to hear the voice that makes all things new.

Let me give a more concrete description of

how the discipline of solitude may be practiced. It is a great advantage to have a room or a corner of a room—or a large closet!—reserved for the discipline of solitude. Such a "ready" place helps us set our hearts on the kingdom without time-consuming preparations. Some people like to decorate such a place with an icon, a candle, or a simple plant. But the important thing is that the place of solitude remain a simple, uncluttered place. There we dwell in the presence of the Lord. Our temptation is to do something useful: to read something stimulating, to think about something interesting, or to experience something unusual. But our moment of solitude is precisely a moment in which we want to be in the presence of our Lord with empty hands, naked, vulnerable, useless, without much to show, prove, or defend. That is how we slowly learn to listen to

God's small voice. But what to do with our many distractions? Should we fight these distractions and hope that thus we will become more attentive to God's voice? This does not seem the way to come to prayer. Creating an empty space where we can listen to God's Spirit is not easy when we are putting all our energy into fighting distractions. By fighting distractions in such a direct way, we end up paying more attention to them than they deserve. We have, however, the words of Scripture to which to pay attention. A psalm, a parable, a biblical story, a saying of Jesus, or a word of Paul, Peter, James, Jude, or John can help us to focus our attention on God's presence. Thus we deprive those "many other things" of their power over us. When we place words from the Scriptures in the center of our solitude, such words—whether a short expression, a few sentences, or a longer text—can function as the point to which we return when we have wandered off in different directions. They form a safe anchoring place in a stormy sea. At the end of such a period of quiet dwelling with God we may, through intercessory prayer, lead all the people who are part of our lives, friends as well as enemies, into his healing presence. And why not conclude with the words that Jesus himself taught us: the Our Father?

This is only one specific form in which the discipline of solitude may be practiced. Endless variations are possible. Walks in nature, the repetition of short prayers such as the Jesus prayer, simple forms of chanting, certain movements or postures—these and many other elements can become a helpful part of the discipline of solitude. But we have to decide which particular form of this discipline best fits us, to which we can remain faithful. It is better to have a daily practice of ten minutes solitude than to have a whole hour once in a while. It is better to become familiar with one posture than to keep experimenting with different ones. Simplicity and regularity are the best guides in finding our way. They allow us to make the discipline of solitude as much part of our daily lives as eating and sleeping. When that happens, our noisy worries will slowly lose their power over us and the renewing activity of God's Spirit will slowly make its presence known.

Although the discipline of solitude asks us to set aside time and space, what finally matters is that our hearts become like quiet cells where God can dwell, wherever we go and whatever we do. The more we train ourselves to spend time with God and him alone, the more we will discover that God is with us at all times and in all places. Then we will be able to recognize him even in the midst of a busy and active life. Once the solitude of time and space has become a solitude of the heart, we will never have to leave that solitude. We will be able to live the spiritual life in any place and any time. Thus the discipline of solitude enables us to live active lives in the world, while remaining always in the presence of the living God.

COMMUNITY

The discipline of solitude does not stand alone. It is intimately related to the discipline of community. Community as discipline is the effort to create a free and empty space among people where together we can practice true obedience. Through the discipline of community we prevent ourselves from clinging to each other in fear and loneliness, and clear free space to listen to the liberating voice of God.

It may sound strange to speak of community as discipline, but without discipline community becomes a "soft" word, referring more to a safe, homey, and exclusive place than to the space where new life can be received and brought to its fullness. Wherever true community presents itself, discipline is crucial. It is crucial not only in the many old and new forms of the common life but also in the sustaining relationships of friendship, marriage, and family. To create space for God among us requires the constant recognition of the Spirit of God in each other. When we have come to know the life-giving Spirit of God in the center of our solitude and have thus been able to affirm our true identity, we can also see that same life-giving Spirit speaking to us through our fellow human beings. And when we have come to recognize the life-giving Spirit of God as the source of our life together, we too will more readily hear his voice in our solitude.

Friendship, marriage, family, religious life, and every other form of community is solitude greeting solitude, spirit speaking to spirit, and heart calling to heart. It is the grateful recognition of God's call to share life together and the joyful offering of a hospitable space where the recreating power of God's Spirit can become manifest. Thus all forms of life together can become ways to reveal to each other the real presence of God in our midst.

Community has little to do with mutual compatibility. Similarities in educational background, psychological make-up, or social status can bring us together, but they can never be the basis for community. Community is grounded in God, who calls us together, and not in the attractiveness of people to each other. There are many groups that have been formed to protect their own interests, to defend their own status, or to promote their own causes, but none of these is a Christian community. Instead of breaking through the walls of fear and creating new space for God, they close themselves to real or imaginary intruders. The mystery of community is precisely that it embraces *all* people, whatever their individual differences may be, and allows them to live together as brothers and sisters of Christ and sons and daughters of his heavenly Father.

I would like to describe one concrete form of this discipline of community. It is the practice of listening together. In our wordy world we usually spend our time together talking. We feel most comfortable in sharing experiences, discussing interesting subjects, or arguing about current issues. It is through a very active verbal exchange that we try to discover each other. But often we find that words function more as walls than as gates, more as ways to keep distance than to come close. Often—even against our own desires —we find ourselves competing with each other. We try to prove to each other that we are worth being paid attention to, that we have something to show that makes us special. The discipline of community helps us to be silent together. This disciplined silence is not an embarrassing silence, but a silence in which together we pay attention to the Lord who calls us together. In this way we come to know each other not as people who cling anxiously to our self-constructed identity, but as people who are loved by the same God in a very intimate and unique way.

Here—as with the discipline of solitude—it is often the words of Scripture that can lead us into this communal silence. Faith, as Paul says, comes from hearing. We have to hear the word from each other. When we come together from different geographical, historical, psychological, and religious directions, listening to the same word spoken by different people can create in us a common openness and vulnerability that allow us to recognize that we are safe together in that word. Thus we can come to discover our true identity as a community, thus we can come to experience what it means to be called together, and thus we can recognize that the same Lord whom we discovered in our solitude also speaks in the solitude of our neighbors, whatever their language, denomination, or character. In this listening together to the word of God, a true creative silence can grow. This silence is a silence filled with the caring presence of God. Thus listening together to the word can free us from our competition and rivalry and allow us to recognize our true identity as sons and daughters of the same loving God and brothers and sisters of our Lord Jesus Christ, and thus of each other.

This example of the discipline of community is one out of many. Celebrating together, working together, playing together —these are all ways in which the discipline of community can be practiced. But whatever its concrete shape or form, the discipline of community always points us beyond the boundaries of race, sex, nationality, character, or age, and always reveals to us who we are before God and for each other.

The discipline of community makes us persons; that is, people who are sounding through to each other (the Latin word *personare* means "sounding through") a truth, a beauty, and a love which is greater, fuller, and richer than we ourselves can grasp. In true community we are windows constantly offering each other new views on the mystery of God's presence in our lives. Thus the discipline of community is a true discipline of prayer. It makes us alert to the presence of the Spirit who cries out "Abba," Father, among us and thus prays from the center of our common life. Community thus is obedience practiced together. The question is not simply, "Where does God lead me as an individual person who tries to do his will?" More basic and more significant is the question, "Where does God lead us as a people?" This question requires that we pay careful attention to God's guidance in our life together and that together we search for a creative response. Here we come to see how prayer and action are indeed one, because whatever we do as a community can only be an act of true obedience when it is a response to the way we have heard God's voice in our midst.

Finally, we have to keep in mind that community, like solitude, is primarily a quality of the heart. While it remains true that we will never know what community is if we never come together in one place, community does not necessarily mean being physically together. We can well live in community while being physically alone. In such a situation, we can act freely, speak honestly, and suffer patiently, because of the intimate bond of love that unites us with others even when time and place separate us from them. The community of love stretches out not only beyond the boundaries of countries and continents but also beyond the boundaries of decades and centuries. Not only the awareness of those who are far away but also the memory of those who lived long ago can lead us into a healing, sustaining, and guiding community. The space for God in community transcends all limits of time and place.

Thus the discipline of community frees us to go wherever the Spirit guides us, even to places we would rather not go. This is the real Pentecost experience. When the Spirit descended on the disciples huddling together in fear, they were set free to move out of their closed room into the world. As long as they were assembled in fear they did not yet form community. But when they had received the Spirit, they became a body of free people who could stay in communion with each other even when they were as far from each other as Rome is from Jerusalem. Thus, when it is the Spirit of God and not fear that unites us in community, no distance of time or place can separate us.

CONCLUSION

Through the discipline of solitude we discover space for God in our innermost being. Through the discipline of community we discover a place for God in our life together. Both disciplines belong together precisely because the space within us and the space among us are the same space.

It is in that divine space that God's Spirit prays in us. Prayer is first and foremost the active presence of the Holy Spirit in our personal and communal lives. Through the disciplines of solitude and community we try to

remove—slowly, gently, yet persistently—
the many obstacles which prevent us from
listening to God's voice within us. God
speaks to us not only once in a while but
always. Day and night, during work and during play, in joy and in sorrow, God's Spirit is
actively present in us. Our task is to allow
that presence to become real for us in all we
do, say, or think. Solitude and community
are the disciplines by which the space
becomes free for us to listen to the presence
of God's Spirit and to respond fearlessly and
generously. When we have heard God's
voice in our solitude we will also hear it in
our life together. When we have heard him
in our fellow human beings, we will also hear
him when we are with him alone. Whether in
solitude or community, whether alone or
with others, we are called to live obedient
lives, that is, lives of unceasing prayer—"un-

ceasing" not because of the many prayers we say but because of our alertness to the unceasing prayer of God's Spirit within and among us.

CONCLUSION

My original questions were, "What
does it mean to live a spiritual life?" and
"How do we live it?" In this book I have
described the spiritual life as the active presence of God's Spirit in the midst of a worry-
filled existence. This life becomes a possibility when, by the disciplines of solitude and
community, we slowly create some free inner
space in our filled lives and so allow God's
Spirit to become manifest to us.

We live in a worry-filled world. We find
ourselves occupied and preoccupied with

many things, while at the same time feeling bored, resentful, depressed, and very lonely. In the midst of this world the Son of God, Jesus Christ, appears and offers us new life, the life of the Spirit of God. We desire this life, but we also realize it is so radically different from what we are used to that even aspiring to it seems unrealistic. How, then, can we move from fragmentation to unity, from many things to the one necessary thing, from our divided lives to undivided lives in the Spirit? A hard struggle is required. It is the struggle to allow God's Spirit to work in us and recreate us. But this struggle is not beyond our strength. It calls for some very specific, well-planned steps. It calls for a few moments a day in the presence of God when we can listen to his voice precisely in the midst of our many concerns. It also calls for the persistent endeavor to be with others in a new way by seeing them not as people to whom we can cling in fear, but as fellow human beings with whom we can create new space for God. These well-planned steps, these disciplines, are the concrete ways of "setting your hearts on his kingdom," and they can slowly dismantle the power of our worries and thus lead us to unceasing prayer.

The beginning of the spiritual life is often difficult not only because the powers which cause us to worry are so strong but also because the presence of God's Spirit seems barely noticeable. If, however, we are faithful to our disciplines, a new hunger will make itself known. This new hunger is the first sign of God's presence. When we remain attentive to this divine presence, we will be led always deeper into the kingdom. There, to our joyful surprise, we will discover that all things are being made new.